Making the most of
BRITISH PORK

Credit to Jackie Lurie and staff at British Meat

INTRODUCTION

British pork, I believe, is one of the most underrated and versatile of meats, lending itself to being cooked in many interesting and creative ways. You can rely on its consistent good quality as well as being lean, moist and succulent and bursting with flavour. It is available all through the year and an extremely good buy, especially for Christmas time.

In this British pork booklet, I have collated a tempting array of inexpensive recipes using well known traditional cuts of British pork from loin chops and spare ribs to lean, tender leg steaks and tenderloin. If you do not recognise a particular joint or cut of British pork (as there are many ways of butchering pork from traditional and regional ways to continental cuts), don't be afraid to ask your butcher for his help and advice on how to cook or prepare it.

Pork is used world-wide in many interesting ways like sweet and sour pork and our traditional roast pork and apple sauce.

With a little flair and imagination you can expand the recipe ideas by adding a few extra ingredients of your own choice.

Throughout the booklet I have given handy tips and advice on cooking and serving ideas, as well as each recipe being calorie counted.

Bon appetit!

Quick and Easy Section
Page 6 to 11

In this section I have used tender lean strips of pork, steaks, lean mince and sausages, that are quick and simple to use as well as being relatively inexpensive. All the dishes have been designed to be cooked and served within 30 minutes.

Lunches and Brunches Section
Page 12 to 23

A range of pork dishes that derive inspiration from French, Italian and Chinese cuisines, as well as from the best traditions of Great Britain. Ideal for the family, or for easy, informal entertaining.

Dinners and Main Meals
Page 24 to 32

New ideas for main meals and dinner parties can be a problem. In this section there are many tempting recipes ranging from Traditional Roast Pork to Pork N' Pineapple Casserole.

Pork N' Pineapple Casserole
Home-Made Raised Pork Pie
Spinach Pork Steaks
Loin of Pork with Lemon and Tarragon Sauce
Roast Pork with Peach, Orange and Ginger Stuffing

Barbecue Section
Page 33 to 39

Barbecues are becoming more and more popular,
and not just for weekend entertaining, whether it
be for friends or family. When marinating, allow
the flavours to absorb into the pork for at least 4-6
hours or, ideally, overnight before cooking over
hot coals or under a hot grill.

Marinades and Basting Sauces
Herb Marinade
Chilli Sauce
Savoury Butters
Pork and Apple Kebabs
Pork on Skewers
Pork Burgers and Barbecue Sauce
Barbecued Spare Ribs

Microwave Section
Page 40 to 48

Pork cooked in the microwave reduces the
cooking times by about one third and brings out
the flavour by cooking in its own natural juices.
When preparing braising cuts of meats, remember
slower cooking and lower settings are required.
Try the tender Fruity Pork Casserole that bursts
with flavour or the Savoury Sausage and Bean Loaf
that is economical to make.

Microwave Guide
Barbecue-Style Spare Ribs
Sweet and Sour Pork Chops
Fruity Pork Casserole
Sausage and Bean Loaf
Pork with Lemon

A really colourful pork dish, full of delicious crunchy vegetables cooked in a rich sauce. If you do not have a wok to cook this dish, a large heavy-based frying pan can be used instead.

Chinese Stir Fry

Serves: 4   Cooking time: 12 minutes

Calories about 280 per portion

1 tbsp oil
1 lb/450g lean pork steaks cut into thin strips
2 cloves garlic, peeled and crushed
1 onion, peeled and sliced
4 oz/100g mushrooms, wiped and sliced
1 small green pepper, de-seeded and cut into
  strips
12 oz/340g can pineapple cubes in natural juice,
  drained
7 oz/175g can water chestnuts, drained and sliced
10 oz/275g bean shoots, rinsed and drained well
Salt and freshly ground black pepper
3 tbsp soy sauce
2 tbsp dry sherry
1 teasp ground cumin

Heat the oil in a wok. Add the pork and garlic, and cook over a high heat, stirring continuously for 5 minutes. Add the onion and stir fry for a further 2 minutes. Add all the remaining ingredients and cook, still stirring, for a further 5 minutes. Serve hot with freshly cooked noodles or fried rice.

Here is a quick recipe which is ideal for lunch or supper, and is economical to make. Use either sweet British tomatoes or the slightly larger ones like beef tomatoes.

Stuffed Tomatoes

Serves: 4   Cooking time: 25 minutes

Calories about 350 per portion

8 large tomatoes (or 4 beef tomatoes)
1 lb/450g lean minced pork
1 onion, peeled and chopped
1-2 cloves garlic, peeled and crushed
1 small green pepper, de-seeded and chopped
1 tbsp tomato purée
1 teasp ground paprika pepper
1 teasp mixed dried herbs
4 tbsp white wine or cider
Salt and freshly ground black pepper

Slice the tops off the tomatoes and reserve. With a teaspoon carefully scoop out the flesh and roughly chop, and discard the seeds. Gently, fry the pork for 5 minutes. Add the remaining ingredients except the tomato shells, and continue to cook for another 5 minutes. Spoon the stuffing into the tomatoes and replace the tops. Place on a baking tray and cook at 180°C, 350°F, Mark 4 for 15 minutes. Serve the tomatoes with your favourite pasta and a fresh green salad.

When grilling, it is always best to preheat the grill for about 3-5 minutes so that the meat is sealed quickly and evenly.

Nutty Pork

Serves: 4   Cooking time: About 15 minutes

Calories about 210 per portion

4 lean pork steaks, ½ inch/1 cm thick
Salt
2 teasp curry paste
1 oz/25g flaked almonds

To garnish:
1 lemon, cut into 8 wedges

Season the steaks lightly with salt and spread evenly on both sides with curry paste. Grill under a moderate heat for 7 minutes each side. Sprinkle one side with almonds and grill until the almonds are golden brown. Serve with lemon wedges.

Double the quantity for an economical main-course meal when entertaining on a budget. Remember, don't prick your chipolata sausages when cooking, as a lot of the flavour will be lost in the juices.

Curried Sausage and Pasta Salad

Serves: 4

Calories about 415 per portion

12 oz/350g pork chipolata sausages, grilled, cooled and cut into ½ inch/1cm pieces
3 oz/75g coloured pasta shapes, cooked and drained well
1 small onion, peeled and very finely chopped
3 oz/75g frozen or fresh peas, cooked
3 oz/75g frozen or fresh sweetcorn, cooked
3 tbsp low calorie mayonnaise or yogurt
1 teasp mild curry paste

Mix the sausages, pasta, onion, peas and sweetcorn. Blend together the mayonnaise and curry paste and mix into the sausages. Chill well before serving.

A firm family favourite, the sweetness of the apple complementing the flavour of the pork.

Pork Steaks with Apple and Green Pepper

Serves: 4   Cooking time: 15-20 minutes

Calories about 300 per portion

2 teasp oil
4 × 5 oz/150g lean pork steaks cut ½ inch/1cm
thick
1 clove garlic, peeled and crushed
4 oz/100g mushrooms, wiped and sliced
1 red eating apple, cored and sliced
1 small green pepper, de-seeded and chopped
¼ pint/150ml unsweetened apple juice
Salt and freshly ground black pepper

Heat the oil in a frying pan and cook the steaks for 12-15 minutes. Remove the steaks from the pan and keep warm. Add the garlic, mushrooms, apple and pepper to the pan and cook over a medium heat for about 1 minute. Pour in the apple juice and boil, uncovered, until reduced and slightly thickened. Season to taste. Pour the sauce over the steaks. Serve with potatoes boiled in their skins, and fresh vegetables.

When time is short and you've a hungry family to feed, this recipe is ideal. Serve the pork slices with freshly cooked plain rice.

Spicy Slices

Serves: 4   Cooking time: About 22 minutes
Calories about 520 per portion
1 lb/450g pork belly slices
1 onion, peeled and chopped
1 tbsp oil
7 oz/200g can tomatoes
15 oz/425g can red kidney beans, rinsed and
*   drained*
2 tbsp tomato purée
1 teasp chilli powder
1 teasp ground cumin
1 teasp ground paprika
1 teasp soft brown sugar
1 tbsp wine vinegar
Salt and pepper

To garnish: *A few sprigs of parsley*

Grill the pork for 6-8 minutes on each side, depending on thickness. Meanwhile, fry the onion in the oil until just soft. Add the rest of the ingredients and cook for 10 minutes. Place the pork slices on a bed of rice and serve the sauce in a separate jug.

An all in one meal containing succulent pieces of pork and lots of fibre gained from two types of beans. Always have handy 1-2 lb/450g-1kg frozen diced pork in the freezer – great for casseroles, kebabs etc.

Pork Cassoulet

Serves: 4   Cooking time: About 1½ hours

Calories about 350 per portion

1 lb/450g lean diced pork
1 onion, peeled and sliced
1 tbsp oil
14 oz/400g can red kidney beans, drained and
    rinsed
7 oz/225g can baked beans
1 teasp chilli powder
Salt
½ pint/300ml stock, from a stock cube
1 tbsp cornflower blended with 2 tbsp cold water

To garnish: *1 tbsp chopped parsley*

Brown the pork and onion in hot oil. Drain well and place in a casserole with the rest of the ingredients except the blended cornflour, and mix well. Cover and put in the centre of the oven at 160°C, 325°F, Mark 3. Cook for about 1½ hours, and stir in the blended cornflour 30 minutes before the end of the cooking time to thicken the sauce. Sprinkle on the parsley and serve with hot rice or noodles.

Bite sized nuggets of pork cooked to perfection in a simple, delicious tomato sauce. Serve on a bed of pasta or with your favourite seasonal vegetables.

Pork Nuggets with Tomato Sauce

Serves: 4   Cooking time: About 45 minutes

Calories about 390 per portion

1 lb/450g lean minced pork
2 carrots, peeled and grated
1 onion, peeled and grated
2 oz/50g fresh wholemeal breadcrumbs
1/2 teasp dried sage or 1 teasp freshly chopped
*   sage*
1 teasp lemon juice
Salt and freshly ground black pepper
1 egg, beaten
2 teasp oil

Sauce:
14 oz/400g can chopped tomatoes
1 onion, peeled and chopped

Place the pork in a large bowl, add the vegetables, breadcrumbs, sage, lemon juice and seasoning and mix together. Mix in the egg. Shape into 16 even-sized balls with dampened hands. Heat the oil in a frying pan and brown the pork nuggets all over. Add the tomatoes and onion. Bring to the boil, cover and cook over a low heat for 30-40 minutes.

This dish makes a pleasant change from the traditional Italian recipe using beef. Choose a make of lasagne that doesn't require any pre-cooking and make sure you drain the spinach very well before using.

Pork and Spinach Lasagne

Serves: 4   Cooking time: About 1 hour

Calories about 300 per portion

1 lb/450g lean minced pork
1 onion, peeled and chopped
2 cloves garlic, peeled and crushed (optional)
4 tbsp dry red wine
4 tbsp stock
4 oz/100g mushrooms, wiped and sliced
1 tbsp tomato purée
1 teasp dried oregano

1 teasp dried mixed herbs
1 × 8 oz/1 × 225g packet frozen spinach, thawed
Salt and freshly ground black pepper
8 sheets lasagne verdi (no pre-cooking required)
½ pint/300ml cheese sauce, made with low fat
   cheese or Quark, and skimmed milk.

Fry the minced pork in a large heavy-based frying pan without adding fat, and heat gently until the pork starts cooking, and the fat runs out. Increase the heat slightly and brown the meat. Drain off any excess fat. Add the onion and garlic and fry until soft. Stir in the wine, stock, mushrooms, tomato purée, herbs, spinach and seasoning. Cook for 2-3 minutes. Layer the meat sauce and lasagne in an ovenproof dish, finishing with a layer of lasagne. Pour the cheese sauce over the top and bake uncovered at 180°C, 350°F, Mark 4 for 40 minutes or until golden brown. Serve with freshly cooked sliced carrots.

A dish that can be served hot or cold to suit our changeable weather. This recipe makes two (4 portion) plaits, one of which may be frozen. But if you are catering for eight people make one large plait.

Pork and Sausage Plait

Serves: 2 × four   Cooking time: 25-30 minutes
Calories about 680 per portion

1½ lb/675g frozen or fresh puff pastry, thawed if frozen
1 lb/450g lean belly pork, finely chopped
1 lb/450g sausagemeat
2 teasp dried basil
Salt and freshly ground pepper
2 eggs, beaten

Roll the pastry into two oblongs about 11 inch × 8 inch/27.5cm × 20cm. Mix the pork with the sausagemeat, basil, seasoning and two thirds of the beaten egg. Form into two 4 inch/10cm rolls and place one down the centre of each piece of pastry, leaving equal borders either side. Gently cut the border obliquely in ½ inch/1cm strips and plait alternate strips over fillings. Glaze the plaits with the remainder of the egg and bake at 220°C, 425°F, Mark 7 for about 25 minutes or until golden. Serve hot with green vegetables, or cold with salad. Let the remaining plait cool thoroughly and freeze as directed below:

To freeze:
Wrap the plait in aluminium foil, sealing the edges well. Overwrap with polythene. Label and freeze.

Storage time:
Up to three months

To thaw:
Thaw overnight in the refrigerator, or re-heat in the oven at the cooking temperature for 40 minutes.

An ideal brunch dish to serve on Sundays. The potatoes may be cooked in a microwave to save time.

Pork and Bean Bakes

Serves: 4   Cooking time: About 1 hour 20 minutes

Calories about 380 per portion

1 lb/450g lean minced pork
4 large baking potatoes, scrubbed well
8 oz/225g can barbecue baked beans
1 oz/25g low fat spread
2 tbsp low fat milk
Salt and freshly ground pepper

Prick the potatoes all over and bake in a pre-heated 220°C, 425°F, Mark 7 oven for about 1 hour or until cooked. A quarter of an hour before the end of the cooking time, put the mince into a saucepan and cook gently until the fat runs out. Increase the heat slightly and continue to cook until the mince is brown. Drain off and discard any fat. Add the baked beans and seasoning and heat gently. Cut the cooked potatoes in half lengthways and carefully scoop out the flesh. Mash the potato with the low fat spread, milk and seasoning. Divide the mince mixture between the baked potato shells and top with mashed potato. Fluff the potato with a fork and place on a baking sheet. Bake in the oven for about 20 minutes at 200°C, 400°F, Mark 6 until brown.

A simple pie that can be prepared in minutes using lean minced pork and a can of baked beans. For extra speed use a good brand of instant potatoes or cooked left-over ones.

Minced Pork and Potato Pie

Serves: 4   Cooking time: 55 minutes

Calories about 220 per portion

1 lb/450g lean minced pork
1 onion, peeled and chopped
15 oz/425g can baked beans
1 teasp Pork Seasoning

1 lb/450g potatoes, peeled and boiled
1 oz/25g low fat spread
2 tbsp low fat milk
Freshly ground black pepper

Fry the minced pork in a large heavy-based saucepan without adding fat, and heat gently until the pork starts cooking and the fat runs out. Increase the heat slightly and brown the meat. Drain off any excess fat, add the onion and fry until the onion is just softened. Add the baked beans and Pork Seasoning. Place the mixture in a shallow ovenproof dish. Mash the potatoes with the low fat spread and mix in the milk. Season with pepper. Top the pork mixture with the mashed potato and fluff up with a fork. Bake at 180°C, 350°F, Mark 4 for 45 minutes until golden. Serve with seasonal vegetables.

This dish will be popular with family and friends. If entertaining, this recipe can be left to cook without any extra attention.

Pork and Red Wine Casserole

Serves: 6   Cooking time: About 1½ hours

Calories about 275 per portion

1 tbsp oil
1½ lb/675g lean diced pork
1 onion, peeled and sliced
8 oz/225g button mushrooms, wiped
2 carrots, peeled and sliced
¼ pint/150ml red wine
½ pint/300ml stock
Salt and freshly ground black pepper
1 tbsp cornflour, blended with 2 tbsp cold water

Heat the oil in a heavy-based saucepan and brown the pork. Add the onion, mushrooms, carrots, red wine, stock and seasoning. Bring to the boil stirring occasionally, cover and simmer for 1¼ hours. Pour in the blended cornflour and stir until thickened. Serve with brown rice or baked jacket potatoes.

Tender pork, cut into thin, uniform-size strips will cook quickly and evenly, as here. Serve with crispy prawn crackers.

Chinese Style Pork

Serves: 4   Cooking time: 15 minutes

Calories about 310 per portion

1 tbsp oil
1 lb/450g pork tenderloin cut into thin strips
1 large onion, peeled and chopped
1 green pepper, de-seeded and chopped
9½ oz/235g can bean sprouts or 8oz/225g fresh
  bean sprouts
4 oz/100g mushrooms, wiped and sliced
3 tbsp soy sauce
4 oz/100g Chinese or thin noodles, cooked and
  drained well
Salt and freshly ground black pepper
3 tbsp dry sherry (optional)

Heat the oil in a large frying pan or wok and fry the pork, onion and pepper for 10 minutes stirring frequently. Add the remaining ingredients, and stir-fry for about a further 5 minutes. Serve immediately onto hot serving plates.

Orange juice and sherry are an excellent combination to enhance the flavour of the pork steaks.

Orange and Sherry Steaks

Serves: 4   Cooking time: 45 minutes
Calories about 285 per portion
4 lean pork steaks
1 green pepper, de-seeded and sliced thinly
1 tbsp cornflour
¼ pint/150ml unsweetened orange juice
1 clove garlic, peeled and crushed
1 tbsp soy sauce
1 tbsp tomato purée
2 tbsp dry sherry
Salt and freshly ground black pepper
To garnish: 1 tbsp orange zest

Place the steaks and green pepper in an ovenproof dish. In a bowl, blend the cornflour with a little of the orange juice. Add the remaining juice and all the other ingredients and mix well. Pour over the steaks and green pepper. Cover and cook in the oven at 160°C, 325°F, Mark 3 for about 45 minutes or until the pork is tender. Serve with brown rice or a green salad.

An excellent way of using left-overs from a roast, Curried Pork Salad makes a nice change from the usual plain cold meats. If you wish, replace the salad cream with low fat Quark or natural yogurt.

Curried Pork Salad

Serves: 4

Calories about 300 per portion

1 lb/450g diced cooked pork
1 red and 1 green apple, cored and diced
2 oz/50g walnut halves
4 sticks celery, finely chopped
½ green or red pepper, de-seeded and chopped
1 small onion, peeled and finely chopped
4 tbsp low calorie salad cream or mayonnaise
*   blended with 1 tbsp curry powder*
Salt and freshly ground pepper
4 oz/100g brown rice, boiled, rinsed and drained
*   well*

Mix well all the ingredients except rice in a large bowl. Arrange on a serving platter with the cold brown or white rice. If you like, cover loosely, and chill briefly, before serving.

Traditional accompaniments for roast pork include roast potatoes, apple or gooseberry sauce, sage and onion stuffing and thickened gravy made from the meat juices.

Roast Pork

Serves: 4-5   Cooking time: 1 hour 45 minutes

Calories about 450 per portion

2 lb/1kg boneless rolled pork joint, with the rind scored
Oil for brushing
Salt

Brush the scored rind with a little oil. Sprinkle with salt and rub it well in. Roast the joint on a grid in a roasting tin in the centre of a pre-heated oven at 180°C, 350°F, Mark 4 for 35 minutes per lb/450g plus 35 minutes.
Do not baste during cooking.

to vary:
Sweet N' Nutty Topping

2 tbsp clear honey
1 tbsp soy sauce
1 clove garlic, peeled and crushed
2 teasp sesame seeds

Blend the topping ingredients together except the sesame seeds. Pour over the joint 30 minutes before the end of the cooking time and sprinkle with the seeds. Return to the oven for the final 30 minutes.

An unusual but mouthwatering combination of pork and fish. Serve piping hot with the rice and diced omelette.

Pork Malayan

Serves: 4   Cooking time: About 30 minutes

Calories about 525 per portion

3 tbsp oil
12 oz/350g lean pork steaks cut into thin strips
6 oz/150g pigs liver, soaked for 1 hour in milk
  then dried and cut into thin strips
1 onion, peeled and finely chopped
2 oz/50g prawns or shrimps, peeled
1 tbsp soy sauce
8 oz/225g long grain rice, boiled and cooled
Salt and freshly ground black pepper
2 eggs
2 tbsp cold water

Heat about one tablespoon of the oil in a heavy based saucepan. Add the pork and cook gently until golden brown. Add the liver and half of the onion and gently cook for 10 minutes, carefully stirring from time to time. Add the prawns and soy sauce, and heat through. Remove from the pan and keep hot. In the same pan heat another tablespoon of the oil and add the rest of the onion and the boiled rice. Season to taste and fry until golden brown. Pile the rice around the edge of a heated serving dish and put the meat mixture into the centre. Keep hot. Beat the eggs and water, and quickly fry an omelette in the remaining oil. Cut into strips and place on top of the meat dish.

Tender shoulder of pork, cooked in a fruity, spicy sauce. Apricots may be substituted for pineapple if liked. Serve with jacket potatoes or brown rice.

Pork N' Pineapple Casserole

Serves: 4   Cooking time: 2 hours

Calories about 390 per portion

1 tbsp oil
1 onion, peeled and sliced
1 green pepper, de-seeded and chopped
1½ lb/675g lean diced pork
8 oz/225g canned pineapple pieces in natural
  juice

3 tbsp soy sauce
2 tbsp sherry
2 tbsp tomato purée
2 tbsp soft brown sugar
2 teasp prepared mustard
½ teasp ground ginger
Salt and freshly ground pepper
1 tbsp cornflour blended with 2 tbsp cold water

Heat the oil in a heavy-based saucepan and lightly fry the onion and green pepper. Add the pork and the other ingredients, except the blended cornflour. Stir well. Bring to the boil. Transfer to a casserole, cover and cook in the oven at 160°C, 325°F, Mark 3 for 1½ hours. Stir in the blended cornflour to thicken the sauce and return to the oven for 15 minutes.

Making a home-made pork pie is certainly worth all the effort. It is an ideal recipe to make for summer eating. To vary the recipe add 1-2 shelled hard-boiled eggs in the middle of the pork mixture before cooking.

Raised Pork Pie

Serves: 12   Cooking time: 2 hours

Calories about 415 per portion

Hot water crust pastry:
1 lb/450g plain flour
1 teasp salt
4 oz/100g lard
1/4 pint/150ml water
2 lb/1kg clean jam jar

*3 lb/1.5kg lean shoulder pork, finely
    chopped or coarsley minced*
*2 teasp fresh sage or thyme or parsley (or a
    mixture of all three)*
Salt and freshly ground black pepper
Milk to glaze
1/4 pint/150ml jellied stock, made from pork bones

To make the hot water crust pastry, sieve the flour and salt into a bowl and make a well in the centre. Heat the lard and water in a pan until just boiling, pour into the flour and mix well with a wooden spoon. When mixture has cooled slightly, turn out onto a lightly floured surface and knead until the pastry is smooth.

Cut off a quarter of the pastry and return this to the warm pan or bowl and keep covered. Flatten out the remaining pastry into a large thick round with a rolling pin. Place a lightly greased jam jar in the centre and work the pastry up the side. It is essential to work quickly as the pastry soon sets, becoming brittle and dry. Allow to cool. Carefully remove the jar. Then refrigerate until the pastry is firm.

Mix the pork, herbs and seasoning and spoon into the pie case. Roll out the remaining pastry to form a lid. Dampen and seal the edges well and glaze with milk. Make a hole in the centre of the pie. Place on a baking sheet and cook for about 2 hours in lower part of the oven at 190°C, 375°F, Mark 5. If the pie becomes too brown, cover loosely with foil. When cooked and cooled, pour in warmed jellied stock through a funnel. (If desired, a pastry rose which has been baked separately can be placed in the centre of the pie, to conceal the hole).

If preferred, use a small cake tin or pie mould bought from a kitchen specialist shop, to shape the pastry.

The lemon and tarragon sauce helps to reduce the richness of the pork.

Loin of Pork with Lemon and Tarragon Sauce

Serves: 6-8   Cooking time: 2¼-2½ hours
Calories about 450 per portion

3½lb-4lb/1.75-2 kg pork loin, chined and scored
1 tbsp oil
1 teasp salt
Sauce:
1 tbsp flour
1 large lemon, grated rind and juice
1 teasp dried tarragon
¼ pint/150ml stock
1 tbsp single cream, top of the milk or thick Greek yogurt

Brush the pork rind with the oil, sprinkle with salt and rub well in. Weigh the joint and roast for 30 minutes per lb/450g plus 30 minutes. Roast at 160°C, 325°F, Mark 3. When cooked, remove the joint from the roasting tin and keep hot. Leave to stand for 10 minutes. Pour off all but 2 tbsp of the juices from the tin, put the tin onto the hotplate and stir in the flour. Cook for 1-2 minutes. Stir in the lemon rind and juice, tarragon and stock to make a smooth sauce. Just before serving stir in the cream. Pour into a sauce boat.

Delicious pork steaks filled with a spinach and oatmeal stuffing.

Spinach Pork Steaks

Serves: 4   Cooking time: 1½ hours

Calories about 465 per portion

4 × 5 oz/125g lean pork steaks cut ½ - ¾ inch/1 - 1.5cm thick
8 oz/225g frozen spinach, cooked and well drained
1 onion, peeled and diced
2 oz/50g medium oatmeal
Salt and freshly ground black pepper
A very little oil
½ pint/300ml stock, made from a stock cube

To garnish: *A little chopped parsley*

Cut a deep pocket lengthwise through the steaks with a sharp knife. Make the stuffing by blending together the spinach, onion, oatmeal and seasoning in a food processor. Stuff the steaks equally with the mixture and secure with cocktail sticks. Brush the steaks with a little oil and place under a preheated grill. Brown both sides quickly, and place in an ovenproof dish. Add the stock and cover tightly. Cook in the oven at 160°C, 325°F, Mark 3 for 1½ hours. Remove the meat and the cocktail sticks and keep hot. Pour the juices into a saucepan and boil to reduce. Pour the sauce over the steaks just before serving. Serve with seasonal vegetables.

British pork is good value all the year as well as being consistent for quality. This recipe is ideal for a lunch time roast.

Roast Pork with Peach, Orange and Ginger Stuffing

Serves: 4-6   Cooking time 30 minutes per lb/450g plus 30 minutes

Calories about 450 per portion

1 onion, peeled and finely chopped
1 peach, skinned, stoned and chopped
1 orange, finely grated rind and juice
Small piece of root ginger, peeled and finely chopped
2 oz/50g fresh breadcrumbs
Salt and freshly ground black pepper
3 lb/1.5kg boned loin of pork
A very little oil
A little salt

Mix the onion, peach, orange zest, ginger and breadcrumbs together. Season well. Add the strained orange juice to bind to make a soft but not sticky stuffing. Spoon the stuffing into the cavity left from the bone and secure the joint with string. Brush the scored rind with the oil and rub in salt. Place in a roasting tin. Roast at 180°C, 350°F, Mark 4 for the calculated time. Do not baste during cooking. Remove the cooked joint from the oven and allow to rest in a warm place for 10 minutes prior to carving. Serve with seasonal cooked vegetables.

Marinades and Basting Sauces

Marinated meats bring variety and exciting tastes to the barbecued foods. You can make marinades easily yourself, or buy them pre-made.

The purpose of a marinade, such as the Herb Marinade that follows, is to moisten, flavour and tenderise meat before it is barbecued. The herbs and flavourings may be varied widely. An acidic element such as lemon or orange juice, wine or vinegar, should always be included, as this helps to ensure the meat's tenderness.

Another way to flavour pork, is to employ a basting sauce-such as the Chilli Sauce that follows. This is brushed over the meat during cooking and is also served with the finished dish.

Herb Marinade

Serves: 6

Makes about ¼ pint/150ml

¼ pint/150ml white wine
2 tbsp wine vinegar
2 tbsp fresh lemon juice, strained
2 tbsp oil
2 tbsp freshly chopped parsley
1 teasp dried mixed herbs
Salt and freshly ground black pepper

Mix all the ingredients together in a bowl or in a screw top jar, and pour over the meat. Cover and leave in a cool place for at least 6 hours, turning the meat occasionally. Ideal for pork and, also lamb.

Chilli Sauce

Serves: 6
Makes about 1/4 pint/150ml
1 small onion, peeled and finely chopped
5 tbsp tomato ketchup
3 tbsp Worcestershire sauce
1 teasp chilli powder
1 tbsp clear honey
1 teasp prepared English mustard
1 teasp oil
Salt and freshly ground back pepper

Mix all the ingredients together in a bowl or a screw top jar to make a smooth sauce. Brush the meat before cooking and several times during cooking. Any remaining sauce can be heated in a saucepan and served as an accompaniment to the finished dish.

Savoury Butters

Just place a little pat of savoury butter on top of the plainly cooked meat to help enhance the flavour.

Lemon and Parsley Butter

Cream together 4oz/100g butter, 1 tbsp freshly chopped parsley, 1 teasp strained lemon juice and seasoning. Refrigerate until well chilled.

Garlic Butter

Cream together 4oz/100g butter, 2 peeled and crushed garlic cloves, 1 tbsp freshly chopped parsley. Refrigerate until well chilled.

Blue Cheese Butter

Cream together 4oz/100g butter and 4oz/100g Stilton. Refrigerate until well chilled.

Tender pieces of pork marinated in a piquant sauce, then cooked in a fruit and vegetable combination.

Pork and Apple Kebabs

Serves: 4   Cooking time: 15-20 minutes
Calories about 390 per portion

Marinade:
2 tbsp soy sauce
2 tbsp clear honey
1 teasp ground ginger
Juice of ½ lemon, strained
1 lb/450g lean pork, cut into 1 inch/2.5cm cubes
*1 green pepper, de-seeded and cut into 1
    inch/2.5cm squares*
2 small onions, peeled and cut into quarters
2 apples cored and cut into quarters
4 mushrooms, wiped and halved

To garnish: *Celery leaves, tomato slices and parsley*

Combine the soy sauce, honey, ginger and lemon juice in a large bowl. Add the pork to the marinade, cover and leave in a refrigerator for 3-4 hours, turning occasionally. Thread the meat, vegetables and apple pieces alternately onto 4 skewers. Place under a hot grill or on a barbecue, turning frequently and basting with the remaining marinade. Serve on a bed of lettuce or boiled rice.

Pork on Skewers

Serves: 2   Cooking time: 15 minutes

Calories about 280 per portion

8 oz/225g pork tenderloin in 1 inch/2.5cm thick
  slices
1 tbsp redcurrant jelly, warmed
1 teasp herb-flavoured mustard
1 tbsp lemon juice, strained
1 tbsp oil
1 tbsp Worcestershire sauce
2 teasp tomato ketchup
Salt and freshly ground black pepper
16 bay leaves
16 pickled onions
Natural yogurt to serve

Mix together the redcurrant jelly, mustard, lemon
juice, oil, Worcestershire sauce, tomato ketchup,
salt and pepper, and pour over meat in a large
bowl; mix well. Cover and leave for 1-2 hours.
Thread pork, bay leaves and onions onto 4 oiled
skewers. Grill or barbecue on foil for about 15
minutes, turning often and brushing with the
remaining marinade. Serve with the reserved meat
juices and, separately, natural yogurt.

If you can't find ready minced pork ask your butcher if he can mince a lean piece of pork for you but do give him a little time. It is a good idea to keep 1 lb/450g in your freezer for emergencies; and the butcher will find a larger quantity easier to mince.

Pork Burgers and Barbecue Sauce

Serves: 4   Cooking time: 20 minutes
Calories about 450 per portion
1 lb/450g lean minced pork
2 oz/50g Sage and Onion Stuffing Mix
2 teasp Worcestershire sauce
Finely grated rind of 1 lemon
1 egg, beaten
Salt and freshly ground black pepper

Sauce:
1 onion, peeled and finely chopped
1/2 oz/15g butter
8 oz/225g canned tomatoes, drained of excess
*   liquid*
1 tbsp malt vinegar
2 tbsp tomato purée
1 tbsp demerara sugar
1 tbsp Worcestershire sauce
2 teasp cornflour, blended with 1 tbsp cold water
Salt and freshly ground black pepper

Mix together the first 6 ingredients. Divide mixture into 8 and shape into burgers. Grill or barbecue for about 10 minutes on each side. Meanwhile, make the sauce: gently cook the onion in the butter in a saucepan until just soft. Add the rest of the ingredients and bring to the boil stirring continuously. Simmer for 10 minutes. Serve with the pork burgers.

Authentic-tasting spare ribs, easy to prepare from start to finish. The secret is to marinade the pork in the spicy sauce for as long as possible, ideally overnight in the refrigerator.

Barbecued Spare Ribs

Serves: 4   Cooking time: 30 minutes

Calories about 305 per portion

2 lb/1kg lean pork spare ribs
1 onion, peeled and finely chopped
1 clove garlic, peeled and crushed
3 tbsp soy sauce

2 tbsp oil
3 tbsp cider vinegar
3 tbsp tomato purée
1 tbsp soft brown sugar
1 teasp five spice powder
Salt and freshly ground black pepper
Put the spare ribs in a shallow dish. Mix the remaining ingredients together in a bowl until smooth and pour over the meat. Cover and leave in a cool place for at least 6 hours, turning occasionally. Grill or barbecue, over a moderate heat turning frequently. If you prefer, bake in an oven at 200°C, 400°F, Mark 6. Serve with a crisp salad.

	COOKING		
Cut	Time per lb (450g) 100% power	Standing Time	Special Points
Leg Fillet end Knuckle	12 mins Cook on 70% power	30 mins	Remove rind before cooking and cook separately under a grill. Turn once.
Loin chops Chump chops	2-6 to 7 mins 4-8 to 10 mins	—	Use browning dish. Turn once
Pork fillet (whole)	8 mins Cook on 70% power.	10 mins	—
Loin and belly (rolled) Leg (rolled)	12 mins	30 mins	Remove rind before cooking and cook separately under a grill. Turn once.
	For cookers with a lower power		

DEFROSTING RAW CUTS		
Time/Power	Standing Time	Special Points
⟩0 mins on 50% power ⟩hen 12 mins per lb on ⟩efrost.	1 hour	Turn once. Protect any part which starts to heat with foil.
⟩ mins on 50% power ⟩hen 12 mins on defrost.	—	Separate after 4 mins. Turn once.
⟩ mins on 50% power ⟩hen 12 mins on defrost.	30 mins	Turn once.
⟩0 mins on 50% power ⟩en 12mins per lb on ⟩efrost	1 hour	Protect any part which starts to heat with foil. Turn once.
⟩vel cook for a few extra minutes.		

All these recipes and charts relate to 650-700 watt microwave ovens. It may be necessary to increase the cooking times to suit your particular model if the output is lower (check with the manufacturer's handbook for guidelines).
The timings for the recipes are based on all the ingredients at room temperature.

Barbecue Style Spare Ribs

Serves: 3-4   Cooking time: 30 minutes

Calories about 420 per portion

2 lb/1kg pork spare ribs
2 tbsp soft brown sugar
3 teasp soy sauce
6 teasp tomato ketchup
Few drops Tabasco sauce

Place the spare ribs in a large shallow dish. Mix together all the other ingredients and pour over the ribs, keeping them in a single layer. Cook uncovered on High, 100% for 30 minutes, turning several times.

Freeze:
In a 2½ pint/1.4 litre casserole

Defrost:
50% for 8 minutes
Stand 10 minutes

Reheat:
75% for 8-12 minutes, uncovered

When buying the spare ribs, do make sure they have plenty of meat on the bones. Serve with a crisp green salad; and don't forget to supply plenty of clean moist napkins or a 'finger-bowl'.

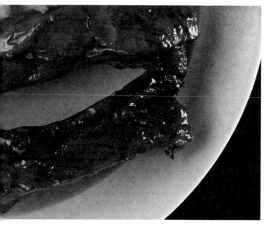

Many Chinese dishes can be complicated, and require many ingredients; but the following recipe is simple, and uses mainly store cupboard ingredients. The pork chops are cooked in a delicious tangy sauce.

Sweet and Sour Pork Chops

Serves: 4   Cooking time: 20 minutes

Calories about 550 per portion

1 onion, peeled and chopped
1 green pepper, de-seeded and chopped
1 carrot, peeled and thinly sliced
1 tbsp cornflour
½ pint/300ml stock, from cube
2 tbsp white wine vinegar
1 tbsp soy sauce
2 tbsp brown sugar
½ teasp ground ginger
Freshly ground black pepper
4 × 6 oz/150g lean pork loin chops,
*   ¾ inch/2cm thick*

Place the onion, pepper and carrot in a bowl and cook on High, 100% for 3 minutes. Stir in the cornflour and the rest of the ingredients (except the chops). Cook on High, 100% for a further 4 minutes stirring once. Remove from the oven. Preheat the browning dish following the manufacturer's instructions. Add the chops and cook on High, 100% for 12 minutes turning after 6 minutes. Drain off any fat then pour the sauce over the chops and cook for a further 1 minute. Season. Serve with jacket potatoes and sweetcorn.

Cooking this dish in the microwave makes the meat very tasty and succulent. The sauce ingredients retain their colour and crisp texture.

Fruity Pork Casserole

Serves: 4   Cooking time: 1 hour 11 minutes

Calories about 500 per portion

1 large onion, peeled and finely sliced
1 large red pepper, de-seeded and finely sliced
1 lb/450g lean pork shoulder, diced
1 clove garlic, peeled and crushed
1 oz/25g flour
2 oz/50g tenderised, stoned prunes
2 oz/50g tenderised, stoned apricots
1/2 teasp dried thyme
1/2 teasp dried marjoram
1/2 pint/300ml stock
4 oz/100g button mushrooms, wiped
Salt and freshly ground black pepper

Put the onion and pepper into a casserole and cook on High, 100% for 4 minutes. Add the meat and garlic and cook on High, 100% for 4 minutes. Stir, then cook for 3 minutes more. Stir in the flour, prunes, apricots, herbs, stock and mushrooms. Season to taste, cover and cook on High, 100% for 10 minutes, then reduce power to 25% and cook for 45 minutes.

Freeze:
In a 2½ pint/1.4 litre casserole
Defrost:
50% for 10 minutes
25% for 15 minutes
Stand for 15 minutes
Reheat:
High 100% for 8-12 minutes.

An economical recipe but do remember when
buying the sausagemeat to choose a high lean
variety. Serve this dish tepid or cold, sliced and
with salad.

Sausage and Bean Loaf

Serves: 6   Cooking time: 17-19 minutes
Calories about 470 per portion
1 lb/450g lean pork sausagemeat
10 oz/275g lean minced pork
1 tbsp Worcestershire sauce
1 tbsp tomato purée
Salt and freshly ground black pepper
Stuffing:
7¾ oz/220g can baked beans
3 oz/75g fresh white or brown breadcrumbs

1 teasp dried mixed herbs
2 tbsp tomato purée

To garnish: *A little lettuce, cucumber and radishes*

Lightly grease a 2 lb/1kg loaf dish. Mix the first five ingredients in a bowl. Press half of this mixture into the base of the dish. Mix all the stuffing ingredients together and spread over the meat mixture in the dish. Add the remaining meat mixture and press down firmly with the back of a metal spoon. Cook on High, 100% for 12-14 minutes. Leave to stand for 5 minutes before turning out.

Freeze:
In a freezer bag, seal and label.

Defrost:
50% for 5 minutes, place strips of foil across end of dish, 25% for 10 minutes.

A really quick dish to make, with a lovely tangy lemon flavour. Serve with hot, freshly cooked pasta.

Pork with Lemon

Serves: 2   Cooking time: 6 minutes
Calories about 325 per portion
12 oz/350g pork tenderloin, in ½ inch/1cm slices
Marinade:
2 tbsp oil
4 tbsp white wine
2 tbsp fresh lemon juice, strained
Salt and freshly ground black pepper
1 bay leaf
Sauce:
1 teasp cornflour
½ teasp ready made mustard
1 tbsp fresh lemon juice, strained
6 tbsp single cream, Quark (natural) or thick
    Greek yogurt
Salt and white pepper

Mix together in a bowl the marinade ingredients. Add the pork, cover and leave for 1 hour. Preheat a browning dish according to the manufacturer's instructions. Remove the slices of pork from the marinade and pat dry on a kitchen towel. Place the pork on the heated browning dish and cook on High, 100% for 2 minutes; turn over and cook for a further 2 minutes. Mix together the sauce ingredients, pour over the pork and stir. Heat for 2 minutes on High, 100%.

Freeze:
In a shallow 1 pint/600ml casserole dish
Defrost:
25% for 6 minutes
Stand for 5 minutes
Reheat:
50% for 4-6 minutes. Reheating on lower power stops the meat from toughening. Stir before serving.